Samuel French Acting Edition

The Gun Show

by E. M. Lewis

Copyright © 2019 by E. M. Lewis
All Rights Reserved

THE GUN SHOW is fully protected under the copyright laws of the United States of America, the British Commonwealth, including Canada, and all other countries of the Copyright Union. All rights, including professional and amateur stage productions, recitation, lecturing, public reading, motion picture, radio broadcasting, television and the rights of translation into foreign languages are strictly reserved.

ISBN 978-0-573-70738-4

www.SamuelFrench.com
www.SamuelFrench.co.uk

FOR PRODUCTION ENQUIRIES

UNITED STATES AND CANADA
Info@SamuelFrench.com
1-866-598-8449

UNITED KINGDOM AND EUROPE
Plays@SamuelFrench.co.uk
020-7255-4302

Each title is subject to availability from Samuel French, depending upon country of performance. Please be aware that *THE GUN SHOW* may not be licensed by Samuel French in your territory. Professional and amateur producers should contact the nearest Samuel French office or licensing partner to verify availability.

CAUTION: Professional and amateur producers are hereby warned that *THE GUN SHOW* is subject to a licensing fee. Publication of this play(s) does not imply availability for performance. Both amateurs and professionals considering a production are strongly advised to apply to Samuel French before starting rehearsals, advertising, or booking a theatre. A licensing fee must be paid whether the title(s) is presented for charity or gain and whether or not admission is charged. Professional/Stock licensing fees are quoted upon application to Samuel French.

No one shall make any changes in this title(s) for the purpose of production. No part of this book may be reproduced, stored in a retrieval system, or transmitted in any form, by any means, now known or yet to be invented, including mechanical, electronic, photocopying, recording, videotaping, or otherwise, without the prior written permission of the publisher. No one shall upload this title(s), or part of this title(s), to any social media websites.

For all enquiries regarding motion picture, television, and other media rights, please contact Samuel French.

MUSIC USE NOTE

Licensees are solely responsible for obtaining formal written permission from copyright owners to use copyrighted music in the performance of this play and are strongly cautioned to do so. If no such permission is obtained by the licensee, then the licensee must use only original music that the licensee owns and controls. Licensees are solely responsible and liable for all music clearances and shall indemnify the copyright owners of the play(s) and their licensing agent, Samuel French, against any costs, expenses, losses and liabilities arising from the use of music by licensees. Please contact the appropriate music licensing authority in your territory for the rights to any incidental music.

IMPORTANT BILLING AND CREDIT REQUIREMENTS

If you have obtained performance rights to this title, please refer to your licensing agreement for important billing and credit requirements.

THE GUN SHOW was developed in the Passage Theatre Lab in Trenton, New Jersey and in Emerging Artists Theatre's One Man Talking Festival in 2013.

THE GUN SHOW was first produced in 2014 at 16th Street Theater in Chicago, Illinois. The artistic director was Ann Filmer, and the director was Kevin Christopher Fox. The cast was as follows:

PLAYWRIGHT................................. Juan Francisco Villa

The solo version of *THE GUN SHOW* was first produced in 2014/2015 at Moving Arts Theater in Los Angeles, California. The artistic director and director was Darin Anthony.

PLAYWRIGHT.. Chuma Gault

CHARACTERS

The **PLAYWRIGHT** is the only character. She should be played by a man somewhere between thirty and fifty. He should be the kind of guy you could cast in a Sam Shepard play. A little bit rough, a little bit soulful, capable of violence.

A note on casting: Both the solo and the duo versions of *The Gun Show* are included in this volume. The solo version of the play requires only a single actor. The role was conceived for a man to play, but you may cast a woman or non-binary actor in this role if desired. In the duo version of the play, the actual playwright – E. M. Lewis – sits out in the audience, and the actor playing the **PLAYWRIGHT** occasionally interacts with her, as indicated in the script. (The duo version of the play is only available for licensing by special request, depending upon the availability of Ms. Lewis to participate.)

SETTING

A bare stage except for a ghost light, a sturdy wooden table, and a sturdy wooden chair.

TIME

Now.

A NOTE FROM THE PLAYWRIGHT

In this volume, you will find two versions of my play *The Gun Show*.

The first version of the play that you'll find here is the "solo" version, which can be done without me. At this printing, the solo version has had more than twenty productions across the country. The second (included as an appendix) is the original version of the play, which I call the "duo" version, in which a male actor tells my story and interacts with me occasionally as I sit out in the audience. I have participated in more than a dozen productions of this version of the play over the last few years, including the world premiere production at 16th Street Theater in Chicago in 2014. I am still available, on occasion, to be part of productions of the play – though only by special request, and depending upon availability.

It was important to me that both versions be included in the same volume so that readers could see how the play was first conceived, but also have a version that they could easily pick up and produce.

The photos mentioned in the play are available from Samuel French upon request.

The play has a certain amount of flexibility in style of presentation, but it's meant to be simple and direct. Without artifice. A table, a chair. An actor, a script. A box full of memories.

This is a true story.

This is my story.

I wish it would stop being so god-damned topical.

~ Ellen

Solo Version

> *(Walk out onstage. The box of photographs and memories is already there, along with the script. Open the script to the first page. Read.)*

Something happened *[number of years since April 27, 2003]* years ago, something...

And I don't know how it can be *[number of years since April 27, 2003]* years, because in my head, it's... right here, loud and bright, like a movie that's always playing, like I live inside the goddamn movie theater, like the movie theater lives inside my head, and there's only one show, there's only ever one show.

But I don't want to talk about that.

> *(Push away from that story like a swimmer pushing away from the side of the pool.)*

Remember that great scene in *Reservoir Dogs*, toward the end of *Reservoir Dogs*, after everything has gone to shit? Mr. Blonde has already done the ear thing with the hostage cop, *Stuck in the Middle with You*, and doused him with gasoline. Mr. Orange is laying there bleeding to death, and he shoots Mr. Blonde, before Mr. Blonde can set the hostage cop on fire. Then the other guys get there with the diamonds, and Mr. Orange tries to tell them Mr. Blonde was going to kill them all and take the diamonds for himself, but Eddie – you remember Eddie? He isn't buying it. He shoots the hostage cop. And then Joe gets there and says *Mr. Orange* is the informant, and Mr. White says no, but Joe points his gun at Mr. Orange, and Mr. White points his gun at Joe, and Eddie points his gun at Mr. White and BOOM, BOOM, BOOM – everybody fucking shoots each other – and it's so surprising, it's hilarious, seriously – and Mr. Pink takes off with the diamonds, and Mr. White crawls over to Mr. Orange and takes him in his arms because everything has gone to shit and he got Mr. Orange into it, but then Mr. Orange says surprise! I totally am the undercover cop, and Mr. White points his gun at Mr. Orange's head, and then the cops are there, finally, but they're not in time, because BOOM.

God, I like that movie. I liked it when I first saw it, and I still like it. But then I look at the goddamn motherfucking news. And I'm starting to not be able to tell the difference between real life and a Tarantino movie.

Everyone has guns in rural Oregon. That's where I grew up.

> *(Look at the box. Pause a moment. Open the box. Rustle around until you find a picture of the playwright's childhood home. Share it with the audience. Smile fondly. Remember.)*

Three shotguns leaned against the wall near our back door. Our neighbors hunted deer up in the mountains every year, and ate what they shot. Most of the men in my family did four years or more in the military, sometimes when there was a war on. The boys at my high school drove pickups, and the pickups had gun racks in the windows, and the gun racks had guns in them. I've shot guns, out in the woods, drinking beer and using the empties as targets.

We had guns, we used guns. They were part of the fabric of our lives in such a way that I didn't even think about them. I didn't think about them any differently than I did about having a toaster or a bicycle. They were useful. They were fun.

But somewhere between there and here and then and now, my feelings about guns have grown more complicated.

Almost everybody I've heard talking about this issue so far is preaching to the converted. If you call something a "Gun Control Theater Action," you are preaching to the choir. If you call your event "Guns Across America," you are preaching to the other choir. I somehow really doubt you're going to have a lot of crossover in audience. I am not putting these events down. I'm just saying, that's not what I'm trying to do here.

What *am* I trying to do here?

> *(Take out a photo of the playwright – E. M. Lewis – and look at it.)*

I am here to tell a public story and a private story. A story about guns in America and a story about my own experiences with guns in America.

Maybe I could have written it as a magazine article or a personal essay, but I don't write magazine articles or personal essays, I write plays.

> *(Beat; smile ruefully, then share the playwright's photograph with the audience, like sharing a secret.)*

I decided not to play myself.

> *(Look at the photo again.)*

I didn't want to do this myself because I'm a coward.

No.

Maybe.

I didn't want to do this myself because I'm not an actor.

I...didn't want to do this myself.

> *(Set the photo on the table.)*

Don't read too much into the fact that I asked a guy to play me. *[Note: change "a guy" to "somebody else" if a female or non-binary actor is playing the role.]* Distance. Just a little distance, that's all it's about. Sometimes you have to take one step back in order to get closer to something.

I usually call everything I write fiction. But I'm calling this one truth. Works the same, though, right? I'm here to tell a story, then leave you to figure out what you think on your own.

Maybe a few stories. With a little talking in between.

Five stories. And you already heard the first one, about how I grew up with guns. And then there's the Learning to Shoot story, and the Jackson's Books story, and the Penn Station story, and the...and one last story to end on.

Five stories.

One down, four to go.

Go.

> *(A moment. Then push forward, right into the thick of it.)*

This show is about GUNS. Did I mention that?

Right now, the whole conversation seems to be between the granola-eating, Whole Foods-shopping, Rachel Maddow-watching, liberal pinko lefties...and the gun-toting, Palin-voting, red-white-and-booyah conservative card-carrying NRA members, as if there is nobody in between who has mixed feelings about the whole thing.

It's a reflection of the greater problem of this whole two-party system of government, which ends up giving us no real choices, only yes or no, this or that, red or blue, freedom or control.

But we don't have time to untangle the problems of the entire U.S. system of government, because I'm talking about GUNS today, and I'm trying to focus.

In 2003, 10,078 people were murdered with guns in America, and 30,135 people were killed with guns, total.

The guns didn't kill the people, though, the people killed the people.

(Look around to see what people think of that.)

Here! You'll like this. *Top Ten Gun Safety Tips.* This is funny. I found it on the internet. I'll just read the first four.

• No matter how excited you are about buying your first gun, do not run around yelling, "I have a gun! I have a gun!"
• Dumb children may get a hold of your guns and shoot each other. If your children are dumb, put them up for adoption to protect your guns.
• If guns make you nervous, drink a bottle of whiskey before heading out to the range.
• Always keep your gun pointed in a safe direction, such as at a hippy or a communist.

Maybe my uncle sent it to me. He was ten years in the Navy and thirty on the highway patrol, and he loves that stuff. "A little bit right of Attila the Hun" is how he describes himself, which I think shows that he has both a little bit of self-awareness and a sense of humor.

He sends me stuff like that – he sends me all kinds of stuff like that – who the hell let our parents' generation onto the internet? But he spent forty years in public service. Navy. Police. Protecting and defending. And despite the tone of a lot of the jokes he e-mails me, I have never, ever seen him act stupidly with guns, and he has never made me feel anything but safe.

Here's something I found from the other side. A political cartoon by Clay Bennett, working for the *Chattanooga Free Press.* It's a picture of the Grim Reaper, holding a newspaper with a front-page headline about soaring gun sales. He's tossing aside his scythe and walking toward a John Deere combine.

Milt Priggee did a cartoon about that Seattle police gun buy-back event where they collected 160 weapons, including assault rifles and a missile launcher. It shows the cops accepting custody of this guy's missile launcher and telling him it's illegal to own a missile launcher. He answers that, if the good guys can't have missile launchers, then only the bad guys will have missile launchers!

I found another one that was pretty good. It said that you should tell the Republicans that the government is trying to take away their math and science textbooks. Then maybe they'll start to hoard those! Ha!

The political cartoon that made the biggest impact on me when I saw it isn't even trying to be funny, though. The title at the top warned that you need to protect your home from killers. Then it just showed a picture of a handgun, surrounded by some statistics. Having a gun in your home triples the risk of a homicide. The vast majority of children who are killed by firearms are killed by a gun that is kept in their own home. People who have a gun in their home are five times more likely to kill themselves. Having a gun in your home increases your chance of being killed by a gun by more than seventy percent.

What went through my head immediately after I read it was, "That can't be right." It doesn't sound right. How can that be right?

But it was exactly what I'd been wanting – less commentary, more facts. Because the commentary is killing the conversation. It feels impossible to even have a conversation about this – I mean a conversation between the two sides, not just more cheerleading and rabble-rousing amongst ourselves.

Do you remember Charlton Heston speaking at that NRA conference, just a year after Columbine?

How about that Piers Morgan, Alex Jones interview, just after a young man murdered twenty children and six adults at Sandy Hook Elementary School in Connecticut?

Gun rights activist Wayne LaPierre, after Parkland?

How about Dana Loesch and that video she did on NRA-TV?

No? Here's a taste.

> *(Step, for a moment, into the persona of a farthest-right pro-gun zealot, like Alex Jones. The following – which doesn't quote any particular person, but reflects a variety of the most extreme pro-gun arguments all mashed together – should begin with reasonable calmness but escalate exponentially in intensity and volume.)*

If those people in that church had guns, they wouldn't have got themselves shot! If those people at that high school had guns, they wouldn't have got themselves shot! People get killed by cars. Are you going to take away the cars? People get killed by getting smashed to death with baseball bats. Are you going to ban baseball bats?

The Second Amendment isn't about hunting. It isn't about duck hunting. It's about protecting ourselves from the tyrannical forces of government! It's about protecting ourselves from criminals who are threatening our families! We are under attack, and they want to take away your right to defend yourself! They want to cut your fucking balls off. This is what it's coming to. This is what it's coming to. We have to stand our ground.

You want my gun? You want my gun? There will be a revolution before you take my gun away. 1776. You want my gun? You just try to come and take it!

> *(Take a moment. Back away from that.)*

This? This is not helping. Because some people listen to this and start stockpiling firearms in their bunkers to protect themselves from the tyrants, and some people listen to this and say if somebody like this can legally buy guns, we're fucked, because he's a nutjob, and where do I sign up for the "Take All the Guns Away Rally"? And there is zero conversation, and zero room for a solution that is somewhere in between.

Some people actually *do* want to take all the guns away. All the swords into fucking ploughshares, Kumbaya.

I don't want all the guns taken away.

>   *(Look at someone out in the audience.)*

Don't look at me like that. You people...

Ha! My father-in-law always says that. "You people."

But seriously. You people who live five seconds away from the police station don't understand the whole situation here. You city people. It's easy for you to say take all the guns away.

When I was growing up...you know how parents teach their kids to call 911? Well, we were supposed to call 911 like everybody else, in case of someone breaking in and trying to rape and kill us all, but then we were supposed to lie and say the house was on fire, because our fire department was local volunteer neighbors who would come in ten or fifteen minutes. The county sheriff was an hour away in Oregon City.

An hour away.

You know what can happen to you in an hour?

What I don't think you people, you good city people, understand is that part of this whole gun control conversation is about people being able to take care of themselves.

No. That's wrong. People not having a fucking choice, because nobody's coming to help you. Help is a million fucking miles away, and you have to choose if you're going to be the kind of person who just lays there and takes it while someone rapes and murders your children right in front of you, or are you going to do something about it?

For those of you who live in close quarters like...you know...*[name of city you're in, or nearest city]*, it's a very different thing when you fire a gun than it is for those of us who are out in the country, because there's another person five feet away from you, and another person five feet away from them, and you have zero control of the bullet once it's out of the chamber. But cities aren't everything. You don't get to own the American story because you live in the city. We count, too. And we understand that it is our own responsibility to defend ourselves.

I own a gun. Did I tell you that?

I didn't buy it for myself. Where I come from, it's the kind of present guys give their womenfolk, after they've been together a while. Paper, cotton, leather, linen, automatic weapons.

Just kidding! That was a joke. It's just a handgun. The kind that fits in your purse. I have it in my purse right now.

Not really.

Inappropriate, I thought, even if this is a gun show.

What I'm saying is, this is a really big country. How often have YOU lived fifty miles away from law enforcement? Think about it. Have you ever?

Then what the fuck do you know about it, and why are you trying to take my fucking guns away?

"You can have my gun when you pry it out of my cold dead hands." John Milius. *Red Dawn*.

That's another good movie. Remember? Commies invade rural America. A bunch of high school kids are forced to take up arms against them. Wolverines!! Patrick Swayze, C. Thomas Howell, Jennifer Grey, Charlie Sheen...

Can you believe Patrick Swayze is dead? God. Sometimes I feel old, just thinking of all the people who seemed like they could never die who are dead now. And if you're sitting there judging me because I put Patrick Swayze on that list, fuck you. He was fucking hot in *Dirty Dancing*.

> (*A moment; shift gears.*)

Where was I?

Me learning to shoot, that's the second story.

> (*Take a picture of Irwin target shooting on the farm out of the box. Remember. Share it with the audience.*)

I went shooting with Irwin out in the woods this one time. Back in Oregon. He wasn't my husband then. Not yet. But we'd been going out a while.

What? You didn't know I have a husband? I have a husband. His name is Irwin. Yes, really. He's a writer too, and he's part of this story.

> (*Pause.*)

It was this perfect Oregon day. You know? Like it was never going to rain again, it was that bright. But everything smelled green, and clean, because it had rained the night before. I was wearing a bikini top and short shorts and ear protection, and we had laid about twenty guns out on a blanket on the grass.

> (*Through the following, you might re-enact the shooting lesson – holding the gun, aiming, having stance corrected, everything.*)

We were down by the lake, on Irwin's folks' place. An old gravel pit, really, but if you dig a hole in Oregon, it's going to fill up with water. Sun glimmered on the water. They'd built a little shooting range down there, years before, against the hillside. Bullet casings were scattered around. Old, ragged paper targets.

Sound of crickets.

We were the only two people in the universe.

Clean, heady smell of his sweat.

I'd never smelled that smell from that close up before.

Irwin was teaching me how to shoot, the real deal, never point your gun at something you don't want dead, telling me where the safety was. We were only drinking a little bit. Only beer.

He put his arms around me and showed me how to focus on the front sight, breathe out, and squeeze the trigger gently. Handguns. Rifles. His grandfather's gun. Guns he'd bought while he was in the Marines. Did I tell you he was a Marine? Oorah, baby. Semper Fi.

I remember that day so clearly. It was so goddamn fun. He knew what he was doing, and what he was doing was strong and masculine and dangerous, and he was letting me in on it, he was giving that to me.

Focus on the front sight.

Breathe out.

Squeeze the trigger gently.

It was louder than anything I'd ever heard before. You nestle the butt of the rifle right up against your shoulder, right here, because it kicks when it fires.

We must have gone through two or three hundred rounds of ammunition that day, and a six-pack or two, in no particular hurry.

That day is bright and perfect in my memory.

Nobody ever made me feel safe like he made me feel safe.

That's the second story.

> *(Take the shirt out of the box – a man's shirt, soft and worn.)*

Raise your hand right now if you've ever held a gun in your hands. If you've ever gone shooting.

> *(Look around at the people who have raised their hands and not raised their hands.)*

If you haven't, you don't know how much fun it can be.

(Put the man's shirt to your face and breathe in. Take a moment. This is a memory you don't want to leave. But everyone is waiting. Put the shirt back in the box.)

Here's the third story.

I was working at Jackson's Books. Small, independent bookstore in Salem, Oregon.

(Turn to the Jackson's Books story in the script. Remember.)

This is how it goes. It's night. It's quiet.

Me and Lauri look in cookbooks for good lasagne recipes.

Some lady calls up. This lady, she's in some contest. A treasure hunt. The question is, "Who wrote 'Pachelbel's Canon'?" So I say it's probably like, "Who's buried in Grant's tomb," but she's not easy about it. "Call me back," I say. "I'll look."

Lauri starts talking some blue-hair into Dostoevsky, I'm sitting on the floor in the music section, and this older guy comes in. And I say, "May I help you?"

He shakes his head and rubs his hands together.

Lauri wraps Fyodor up in blue paper behind the counter.

My guy looks a little lost over in Lit. Crit., so I say, "Is there anything I can help you find?"

"Is there anything you got in horr..." he says.

"Excuse me?" I say.

"Horrerrrr," he says a little louder. "Horror."

"Oh, sure," I say.

He's not telling any names, so I say, "How about Stephen King?" I hand him *Misery*, and *It*.

He thumbs through them kind of fast, like he's forgot his glasses. Blue-hair's gathering her stuff.

"You got...um...*Flowers in the Attic*, something like that?" he says.

"V.C. Andrews," I say. "Right down here."

The door clangs shut.

"I'll take them," he says, handing me all three of the paperbacks.

I go around the side of the counter. Lauri's still standing over at the other register. I scan each of the books, then look at the total. It says $14.97.

"Fourteen ninety-seven," I say, and look up.

And there is a really big black gun pointed at me.

Well, I really can't say how big it was. It looked like a bazillion caliber gun with its opening pointed right toward me. The cops told me later, laughing, any gun that's pointed at you looks big.

I just stood there. One hand poised over the register, the other hovering over the books on the counter.

And suddenly, my mind slips me out from the body that sees that gun pointed at me to some place hovering up above and watching. And the expression that girl (who is me) has on her face is just like that big-eyed look that deers have when they're caught, for that one horrible moment, in your headlights.

"...Down on the floor," you hear him say. He's looking at Lauri.

"Down on the floor. Get down on the floor." By the third time he says this, he's shouting.

Lauri is just standing there, with those same deer eyes you have. Come to find out later, she couldn't even see the gun, with all the stuff on the counter. She did know though. She didn't understand what was going on, but she knew.

Lauri tells you later that you told her "It's okay" at this point, and that it was only when you said that to her that she crouched down behind the counter. She curled her arms around herself, like a kid under a desk when the bomb siren goes off.

"Get the money out of the register," he says to you. "Get The Money Out Of The Register! GET THE MONEY OUT OF THE REGISTER!!"

He pulls a crumpled brown paper bag out of his jacket and throws it on the counter. It slides across, and falls lightly to the floor.

"Get the bag – Get The Bag – GET THE BAG," he says, and his eyes are wide and fierce and the gun is pointed at you still.

You feel yourself moving, looking down at Lauri, picking up the bag.

The drawers at Jackson's won't come open again if you shut them, so they are always left ajar. We are woefully unprepared for this. You pull out the drawer in front of you.

Your fingernails slip on the bills in the cash register and you can't get hold of them.

"HurryupHurryUpHURRYUP!!" the man shouts.

You get your fingers around the corners of the bills, somehow, your fingernails making scraping sounds on the paper, and you think, "My God, I'm going to be killed because I didn't cut my fingernails."

You put the money in the bag and you put the bag on the counter and he shoves the bag back toward you.

"Gettheotherregister! GetTheOther…"

You step around Lauri, careful not to step on her hands, which she has set on the ground in front of her to keep her balance.

The man's hands are shaking, as he holds the gun, and as you empty the second register, you understand that if he doesn't shoot you on purpose, he may just shoot you accidentally. There is a tightness in your throat. Your own hands begin to shake, almost uncontrollably.

You push the bag of cash toward him, and he shoves it in his jacket.

He gestures at you with the gun.

You back away from the counter.

"Down on the floor. Down On The Floor. Get DOWN ON THE FLOOR!"

You get down on the floor, on your knees, on the dirty gray carpet.

The man's voice comes from the other side. "You count to a hundred," he says.

After a pause, you hear the door fall shut.

You will never know who moved first, but then you and Lauri are grasping each other's hands. You have never felt so close to anyone in your life as in that moment.

You don't count, but a little after the door sounds like it closes, you and Lauri look at each other, then cautiously get up, peering over the counter. There is a man there, but it is just some guy with brown hair and loafers, paging through a book from the "New Non-Fiction" display by the door. He doesn't notice the two of you, rising up from behind the counter like ghosts.

Things get kind of fuzzy, there for a while. You sit down on the stool behind the counter.

Lauri asks the man in the loafers if he saw the guy who just went out. The guy had no clue what had just happened. He was shocked. He'd passed right by the man, not even knowing it.

Lauri does all the right things. Locking the front door and calling the police. She had been a bank teller, and had the training.

You just sit there, kind of breathless.

The police come. Neither of the owners were home when Lauri called, but the manager and her husband come. Her husband is a retired English professor, and he keeps asking you questions like Columbo or Poirot, "Did he give off any peculiar smells? Did he have a tattoo?" even after the police stop.

The policeman is standing beside you, though, when you see your husband, framed in the glass doorway. He has a rose in rumpled green paper in one hand, and a box from the lingerie place in the other. Because it is your birthday. You are twenty-five.

There is a blank look in Irwin's eyes, as he pauses there in the doorway, waiting for Lauri to unlock it with her jingling ring of keys, knowing that something has gone wrong. You look over the shoulder of the policeman at him apologetically.

You finally get to sleep that night after the sun comes up. After getting drinks at Thompson's with Lauri, just till you quit shaking so bad. Your husband says it's the adrenaline – it's natural.

People say kind things and they say awful things. You remember the awful things best. Your boss, who has been taking judo with his sons at the same place you learned the little bit you know, asks you if you thought of using it, when "it happened." You want to bash his face in. It increases the guilt you feel that you could let this happen to you. One of the girls we work with tells Lauri, when Lauri says how afraid she is that the man is out there still, that "it's not like he raped you or anything." Lauri goes in the back, into the bathroom, and cries.

You go on, though. You keep working the evening shift, even though your mind goes back to that, now. The robbery. And it is harder to be friendly to strangers. You had sometimes been afraid, before, and now you are, sometimes, not afraid. You do go on, though.

But as you write this, putting words to paper, words run through your head.

I will never be the same.

I will never be the same.

I will never be the same.

That was the third story.

Note that no bookstore cashiers were actually hurt during this incident.

> *(Take the picture of young Ellen in her Jackson's Books days and share it.)*

Everybody was fine.

I'm totally fine.

I'm totally fine.

So what makes me feel like I need to stand up here and talk about this?

All you're seeing are the freaks. All anybody is seeing on the news are the freaks, people who really DO want to take all the guns away, or flag-draped yahoos like Alex Jones, when the reality is...

Somewhere between forty and forty-five percent of all households in America own guns, and they're not all nutcases who secretly want to gun us all down in a movie theater or a post office or a grade school. Somewhere between fifty-five and sixty percent of all households in America DON'T own guns, and they're not all pansy-ass granola-eating hippies who would rather stand and watch their family raped and killed than defend themselves.

There is a conversation to be had, here, that's not happening, it's been stolen from us sensible, relatively reasonable, regular sort of people in the middle, and the middle is bigger than the edges, we are way bigger than them, they just strut better, like fucking peacocks

– but I aim to take this conversation BACK, because it belongs to us, all of us, and I refuse to cede this ground to the nutjobs who don't want to let us talk to each other, because we're the kind of people who might admit that this issue has just a little bit of fucking complexity to it. And that we have more in common with each other than we have that separates us.

We are human. We breathe air. We live in the world. We eat, we drink, we require shelter. We crave companionship. We build families.

We want to be SAFE.

I've been thinking about this gun thing a lot, circling around it.

And what I think it comes down to, this gun thing, is safety. That's what we have in common. We want to be *safe*.

Fourth story.

(Take out the New York City subway map.)

So I've just moved to New Jersey from Los Angeles, where there is no public transportation – well, no public transportation that makes a dent in the vast distances you're always having to go, it's fifty-five miles across, the city of Los Angeles, did you know that? Manhattan is two point three miles across.

I've moved to New Jersey, but today I've taken the train into New York City, which feels much more like a city than Los Angeles ever will, and I've spent the day there, getting lost no fewer than three times, and looking at my little map like the newbie I am.

It's dark and rainy and cold out, and I'm exhausted, and it's late, and I'm in Pennsylvania Station, which smells like urine and is constantly, constantly under construction. I'm looking for New Jersey Transit, because I know that's what I need to get home.

There are these two cops standing there in the station, and so I go over and ask them which way to the New Jersey Transit trains, and the big, broad-shouldered, white cop, whose hand rests firmly and comfortably on his sidearm, says, "I'm gonna pistol-whip the next asshole from New Jersey who fuckin' asks me that, read the fuckin' signs." And the big, broad-shouldered, younger Latino cop standing beside him doesn't say anything.

The cop's hand doesn't move from his sidearm. His hand doesn't move. But I am suddenly aware of his hand, resting firmly and comfortably on the butt of his gun, the silver snap on the black leather holster that can be flicked open with his thumb as he draws the gun out of the holster, and he doesn't do that, he doesn't, but I'm very aware of his large, calloused hand.

He never would have said that to me if I was...if I was with Irwin.

Funny thing, how if you have a gun, your tendency is to use it.

(Beat; tilt head. No, that's not right.)

He didn't use it. He didn't draw. He didn't fire. He just...

They always say that thing, though. And I think there's something to it. If you ask a pharmacist what to do, they'll prescribe a pill. If you ask a surgeon, the only thing to do is cut it out. If you have a gun...

(Beat.)

It wasn't really even a threat. Not really. He didn't move when he said it. But I guess it's another one of my gun stories.

I found New Jersey on my own.

I like cops. My uncle is a cop. Cops make me feel...

(Pause.)

One more story.

Do I tell it?

Do I tell it?

Something happened *[number of years since April 27, 2003]* years ago, something...

And I don't know how it can be *[number of years since April 27, 2003]* years, because in my head, it's...

The trouble is that the closer I come to telling *this* story, saying the absolute truth, unvarnished, unadorned, the closer I come to having a panic attack. I mean the head between my knees, gasping like a fish in the fucking cereal aisle kind.

Maybe I'll just tell you four stories today. Leave it at that.

> *(Look at the picture of the playwright.)*

If not now, when?

Something happened *[number of years since April 27, 2003]* years ago.

April 27, 2003.

This is the first story, this is the last story, this is the only story.

> *(Take Ellen and Irwin's wedding picture out of the box and look at it, then share it with the audience. Smile. Remember. Let this story be happy until it isn't, okay?)*

Irwin and I were the only married couple in our grad school writing program. You remember Irwin from the Learning to Shoot story, right? Met him when I was nineteen and he was twenty-nine, and everything was shining ahead of us. Met him and married him back in Oregon, then went off to grad school together to be Writers, capital W. And everybody in our program would come over to our place, and I'd cook, and we'd drink, and we'd share our writing and talk long into the night, like grad school is supposed to go. Then grad school was done with, and we went out into the real world. And he got a crazy job in the internet boom just in time to ride it all the way up, then all the way back down to the internet bust. And I found a job just as we were getting to absolute zero, but he didn't. And he didn't. And he didn't. And he kind of stopped looking after a while, and he kind of got anxious and depressed.

(Beat.)

Irwin's the toughest guy I ever met, Marine Corps, oorah, put himself through college working as a correctional officer, ran a marathon, tough, and he's always the funniest guy in any room he's in. He's the fucking sun, and most of the time I was happy to be a planet, because of the brightness and the warmth. He's the toughest guy I ever met. So it took about two years of shrinks and pills and VA counselors and sometimes walking all night together through the Los Angeles dark, where there are no stars, only airplanes, because he was feeling nervous, all of which we didn't really tell anybody about, because he didn't want anybody to know –

– Shh! Don't tell anybody, don't tell anybody, don't tell anybody, don't leave me, don't let them take me away some place, don't you fucking tell anybody, please don't leave, baby, shh!

– Before he took a beautiful shiny black Glock and put it in his mouth and pulled the trigger. And when I found him, he was... And when I found him, he was...

There's not really any doubt when someone uses a gun. Because you can see that he's... Blood on the...concrete floor of the...not-blood on the... Red and gray. Red and gray. Red and gray. I put my hand on his chest. Then I put my ear to his chest, too...because...I, uh...couldn't... I still can't, really...believe that...

(Pause.)

He was really funny. You would have liked him.

Nineteen thousand, one hundred and thirty-four people killed themselves with guns in 2003. Plus one. Nineteen thousand, one hundred and thirty-five.

I'm the kind of widow you don't talk about, because there's a shame in suicide. There's a god-awful guilt, because if you love someone, you're not supposed to let them down, and if they're dead... You failed.

But if we don't talk about this, if we don't talk about suicide, we're skipping a huge part of the story. The guns-make-you-safe story.

I don't want to take everybody's guns away. But I sure wish I'd manned up and taken his guns away.

We have met the enemy, and he is us.

All the people I know who have died from guns killed themselves.

- Mr. Stone, my high school biology teacher.
- Kid I went to catechism classes with, who also happened to be my seventh-grade teacher's son.
- Ron, a friend of my aunt and uncle.
- Richard's dad.
- Irwin.
- Hunter S. Thompson.
- Ernest Hemingway.

And don't you try to tell me I can't have those last couple guys because I didn't know them, I fucking love those guys.

Is my list shorter or longer than yours?

I don't know anybody who has ever drawn a gun to protect themselves. Maybe my father-in-law did, in Korea. I don't know. He doesn't talk about it.

Guns don't equal safety.

"No guns" doesn't equal safety.

There is no fucking safety.

You can call me an asshole or an idiot, because after all that I don't want to take everybody's guns away. I'm still the Oregon farm girl who grew up with a .22 leaning in the corner by the back door, who understands that there are people who should have a few guns and places where they are practical and useful tools.

You can call me an asshole or an idiot, because one particular incident made me think we need to talk about guns, and bring the facts about them out into the open. The main fact I'm talking about being that if there's a gun in your house, you're more likely to shoot yourself with it than protect yourself with it.

You can say "that wouldn't be me" all you'd like. I never thought it would be Irwin. I never thought it would be, right up until it was. And I know I'm not alone.

(Beat.)

I never tell this story.

I shoved both of us in a box and put us away. And now it's *[number of years since April 27, 2003]* years later – and here we are. Still in the same box I put us in. I can put us back in. I can do it. I'm good at this. But that doesn't get us anywhere, does it?

Irwin killed himself. He certainly could have killed me. I have wondered if he thought about it. I kept the gun he gave me. Just in case I ever wanted to…write a play about guns.

(A moment.)

Irwin and I are locked together forever. Death didn't part us. For *[number of years since April 27, 2003]* years, I've held him tight and close, right here.

(Clench fist and press it against side, against the lowest and most vulnerable ribs.)

The tighter my hold, the more caught I am.

It's like how you catch a monkey. I read about this somewhere. It's easy. Apparently. I've never been to any place with wild monkeys to try it out. But they say that all you have to do is drill a small hole in a gourd and tie it to a tree. Put a piece of fruit inside. Then come back later to see if you've caught one. What happens is they smell the sweet fruit and stick their hand through the hole and grab it. Their little fists won't fit back through the hole, but they won't let go. You can go back any time you want. They'll still be there, clutching tight. You can just scoop them up in a bag, and there you go.

We have guns, and the guns have us. We're scooping ourselves up in shiny black body bags.

You're just as stuck as I am, America. In love with something that's hurting us and not sure how to separate it from our identity. America means freedom and liberty and self-determination and independence, and guns were a tool we used to get those things, one of the tools, they were, but they weren't the point. The freedom was the point. And I don't think we're very free right now.

We're afraid. All of us. And we aren't talking to each other.

If you're on the right, do you feel like you can talk about a few simple, practical things we might want to do to keep guns out of the hands of people who shouldn't have them – like three-year-olds and convicted felons and maybe the mentally ill? Or is that unacceptable? Who says?

If you're on the left, do you feel like you can talk about the times and places where guns might be a practical tool for hunting or self-defense? Or even just fun, like some of the other dangerous things we love sometimes? Or is that unacceptable? Who says?

Can we have this conversation? If not, why not? What's stopping us from figuring this out? I know it's complicated. But we are in this together. This country. This society. This community.

Me and Irwin's story – is just one story, one gun story in a country full of gun stories and a lot of them are a lot more…but this one is mine. And I don't want to be silent about it anymore. I failed before. I don't want to fail again. So I'm not going to put us back in the box.

> *(A moment.)*

I haven't given you a plan, here tonight. Actions to be taken. Congressmen to be called. Protests to carry signs at.

All I have to give you is the story I never tell.

> *(Take a handful of pages from the script and give them to a few random audience members.)*

Here. Here.

Take this. Here. Take it.

> *(A moment…and then look across at the box of memories. Walk over and put your hand on the wedding photo. Maybe now, you can finally let your story go. And have it back. And go on.)*

If I give our story out to enough people, maybe I'll never be able to put us back in.

> *(Go to the door of the theater. Open the door of the theater. Step out into the world.)*
>
> *(A moment. Then the lights go out.)*

End of Play

Appendix: Duo Version

The inclusion of this version is a dramaturgical gesture designed to act as a resource for licensees of the Solo Version. To perform this version, interested parties must contact their Samuel French licensing agent for further information. The Duo Version is not available for performance without the participation of the playwright, E. M. Lewis.

(Walk out onstage. Find the script there on the table, and the box. Open the script to the first page. Read.)

Something happened *[number of years since April 27, 2003]* years ago, something...

And I don't know how it can be *[number of years since April 27, 2003]* years, because in my head, it's...

(Close and open your hand near your head.)

Right here, loud and bright, like a movie that's always playing, like I live inside the goddamn movie theater, like the movie theater lives inside my head, and there's only one show, there's only ever one show.

But I don't want to talk about that.

(Push away from that.)

(A moment. Then look out at the audience and talk with them. Have fun with this bit!)

Remember that great scene in *Reservoir Dogs*, toward the end of *Reservoir Dogs*, after everything has gone to shit? Mr. Blonde has already done the ear thing with the hostage cop, *Stuck in the Middle with You*, and doused him with gasoline. Mr. Orange is laying there bleeding to death, and he shoots Mr. Blonde, before Mr. Blonde can set the hostage cop on fire. Then the other guys get there with the diamonds, and Mr. Orange tries to tell them Mr. Blonde was going to kill them all and take the diamonds for himself, but Eddie – you remember Eddie? He isn't buying it. He shoots the hostage cop. And then Joe gets there and says *Mr. Orange* is the informant, and Mr. White says no, but Joe points his gun at Mr. Orange, and Mr. White points his gun at Joe, and Eddie points his gun at Mr. White and BOOM, BOOM, BOOM – everybody fucking shoots each other – and it's so surprising, it's hilarious, seriously – and Mr. Pink takes off with the diamonds, and Mr. White crawls over to Mr. Orange and takes him in his arms because everything has gone to shit and he got Mr. Orange into it, but then Mr. Orange says surprise! I totally am the undercover cop, and Mr. White points his gun at Mr. Orange's head, and then the cops are there, finally, but they're not in time, because BOOM.

God, I like that movie. I liked it when I first saw it, and I still like it. But then I look at the goddamn motherfucking news.

And I'm starting to not be able to tell the difference between real life and a Tarantino movie.

(Pause.)

Everyone has guns in rural Oregon. That's where I grew up.

(Look at the box. Pause a moment. Open the box. Rustle around until you find a picture of the playwright's childhood home. Share it with the audience. Smile fondly. Remember.)

Three shotguns leaned against the wall near our back door. Our neighbors hunted deer up in the mountains every year, and ate what they shot. Most of the men in my family did four years or more in the military, sometimes when there was a war on. The boys at my high school drove pickups, and the pickups had gun racks in the windows, and the gun racks had guns in them. I've shot guns, out in the woods, drinking beer and using the empties as targets.

We had guns, we used guns. They were part of the fabric of our lives in such a way that I didn't even think about them. I didn't think about them any differently than I did about having a toaster or a bicycle. They were useful. They were fun.

But somewhere between there and here, and then and now, my feelings about guns have grown more complicated.

Almost everybody I've heard talking about this issue so far is preaching to the converted. If you call something a "Gun Control Theater Action," you are preaching to the choir. If you call your event "Guns Across America," you are preaching to the other choir. I somehow really doubt you're going to have a lot of crossover in audience. I am not putting these events down. I'm just saying, that's not what I'm trying to do here.

What *am* I trying to do here?

I am here to tell a public story and a private story. A story about guns in America and a story about my own experiences with guns in America.

And when I say my experiences, I mean hers.

> *(Pick up the flashlight and use it to point out the playwright, E. M. Lewis, who is sitting out in the audience. Feel free to go right up to her. Then, to both the audience and the playwright, like sharing a secret:)*

I decided not to play myself.

I didn't want to do this myself because I'm a coward.

No.

Maybe.

I didn't want to do this myself because I'm not an actor.

I...didn't want to do this myself.

> *(Take the flashlight off the playwright.)*

Maybe I could have written it as an essay, but I don't write essays, I write plays, and make actors say the words for me.

The trouble is that the closer I come to telling *this* story, saying the absolute truth, unvarnished, unadorned, the closer I come to having a panic attack. I mean the head between my knees, gasping like a fish in the fucking cereal aisle kind.

(Gesture to someone in the front row.)

You know what I'm talking about.

(Look away from that person but then look back again, giving some weird hand gesture of solidarity.)

Don't read too much into the fact that I asked a guy to play me.

Distance. Just a little distance, that's all it's about. Sometimes you have to take one step back in order to get closer to something, and I'm...uh...getting pretty close with this one.

I usually call everything I write fiction. But I'm calling this one truth.

Works the same, though, right?

I'm here to tell a story, then leave you to figure out what you believe on your own.

Maybe a few stories. With a little talking in between.

Five stories. And you already heard the first one, about how I grew up with guns. And then there's the Learning to Shoot story, and the Jackson's Books story, and the Penn Station story, and the...and one last story to end on. Five stories.

One down, four to go.

Go.

This show is about GUNS. Did I mention that?

Right now, the whole conversation seems to be between the granola-eating, Whole Foods-shopping, Rachel Maddow-listening, liberal pinko lefties...and the gun-toting, Palin-voting, red-white-and-booyah conservative card-carrying NRA members, as if there is nobody in between who has mixed feelings about the whole thing.

It's a reflection of the greater problem of this whole two-party system of government, which ends up giving us no real choices, only yes or no, this or that, red or blue, freedom or control.

But we don't have time to untangle the problems of the entire U.S. system of government, because I'm talking about GUNS today, and I'm trying to focus.

In 2003, 10,078 people were murdered with guns in America, and 30,135 people were killed with guns, total.

The guns didn't kill the people, though, the people killed the people.

> *(Look around to see what people think of that.)*

Here! You'll like this. *Top Ten Gun Safety Tips*. This is funny. I found it on the internet. I'll just read the first four.

• No matter how excited you are about buying your first gun, do not run around yelling, "I have a gun! I have a gun!"

• Dumb children may get a hold of your guns and shoot each other. If your children are dumb, put them up for adoption to protect your guns.

• If guns make you nervous, drink a bottle of whiskey before heading out to the range.

• Always keep your gun pointed in a safe direction, such as at a hippy or a communist.

Maybe my uncle sent it to me. He was ten years in the Navy and thirty on the highway patrol, and he loves that stuff. "A little bit right of Attila the Hun" is how he describes himself, which I think shows that he has both a little bit of self-awareness and a sense of humor.

He sends me stuff like that – he sends me all kinds of stuff like that – who the hell let our parents' generation onto the internet? But he spent forty years in public service. Navy. Police. Protecting and defending. And despite the tone of a lot of the jokes he e-mails me, I have never, ever seen him act stupidly with guns, and he has never made me feel anything but safe.

Milt Priggee did a cartoon about that Seattle police gun buy-back event where they collected 160 weapons, including assault rifles and a missile launcher. It shows the cops accepting custody of this guy's missile launcher and telling him it's illegal to own a missile launcher. He answers that, if the good guys can't have missile launchers, then only the bad guys will have missile launchers!

I found another one that was pretty good. It said that you should tell the Republicans that the government is trying to take away their math and science textbooks. Then maybe they'll start to hoard those! Ha!

The political cartoon that made the biggest impact on me when I saw it isn't even trying to be funny, though. The title at the top warned that you need to protect your home from killers. Then it just showed a picture of a handgun, surrounded by some statistics. Having a gun in your home triples the risk of a homicide. The vast majority of children who are killed by firearms are killed by a gun that is kept in their own home. People who have a gun in their home are five times more likely to kill themselves. Having a gun in your home increases your chance of being killed by a gun by more than seventy percent.

What went through my head immediately after I read it was, "That can't be right. It doesn't sound right. How can that be right?"

But it was exactly what I'd been wanting – less commentary, more facts. Because the commentary is killing the conversation. It feels impossible to even have a conversation about this – I mean a conversation *between* the two sides, not just more cheerleading and rabble-rousing amongst ourselves.

Do you remember Charlton Heston speaking at that NRA conference, just a year after Columbine?

How about that Piers Morgan, Alex Jones interview, just after a young man murdered twenty children and six adults at Sandy Hook Elementary School in Connecticut?

Gun rights activist Wayne LaPierre, after Parkland?

How about Dana Loesch and that video she did on NRA-TV?

No? Here's a taste.

> *(Step, for a moment, into the persona of a farthest-right pro-gun zealot, like Alex Jones. The following – which doesn't quote any particular person, but reflects a variety of the most extreme pro-gun arguments all mashed together – should begin with reasonable calmness but escalate exponentially in intensity and volume)*

If those people in that church had guns, they wouldn't have got themselves shot! If those people at that high school had guns, they wouldn't have got themselves shot! People get killed by cars. Are you going to take away the cars? People get killed by getting smashed to death with baseball bats. Are you going to ban baseball bats?

The Second Amendment isn't about hunting. It isn't about duck hunting. It's about protecting ourselves from the tyrannical forces of government! It's about protecting ourselves from criminals who are threatening our families! We are under attack, and they want to take away your right to defend yourself!

They want to cut your fucking balls off. This is what it's coming to. This is what it's coming to. We have to stand our ground.

You want my gun? You want my gun? There will be a revolution before you take my gun away. 1776. You want my gun? You just try to come and take it!

(Beat.)

This? This is not helping. Because some people listen to this and start stockpiling firearms in their bunkers to protect themselves from the tyrants, and some people listen to this and say if somebody like this can legally buy guns, we're fucked, because he's a nutjob, and where do I sign up for the "Take All the Guns Away Rally"? And there is zero conversation, and zero room for a solution that is somewhere in between.

Some people actually *do* want to take all the guns away. All the swords into fucking ploughshares, Kumbaya.

I don't want all the guns taken away.

(Look at someone out in the audience.)

Don't look at me like that. You people...

Ha! My father-in-law always says that. "You people."

But seriously. You people who live five seconds away from the police station don't understand the whole situation here. You city people. It's easy for you to say take all the guns away.

When I was growing up...you know how parents teach their kids to call 911? Well, we were supposed to call 911 like everybody else, in case of someone breaking in and trying to rape and kill us all, but then we were supposed to lie and say the house was on fire, because our fire department was local volunteer neighbors who would come in ten or fifteen minutes. The county sheriff was an hour away in Oregon City.

An hour away.

You know what can happen to you in an hour?

What I don't think you people, you good city people, understand is that part of this whole gun control conversation is about people being able to take care of themselves.

No. That's wrong. People not having a fucking choice, because nobody's coming to help you. Help is a million fucking miles away, and you have to figure out if you're going to be the kind of person who just lays there and takes it while someone rapes and murders your children right in front of you, or are you going to do something about it?

For those of you who live in close quarters like...you know...*[name of city you're in, or nearest city]*, it's a very different thing when you fire a gun than it is for those of us who are out in the country, because there's another person five feet away from you, and another person five feet away from them, and you have zero control of the bullet once it's out of the chamber. But cities aren't everything. You don't get to own the American story because you live in the city. We count, too. And we understand that it is our own responsibility to defend ourselves.

I own a gun. Did I tell you that?

I didn't buy it for myself. Where I come from, it's the kind of present guys give their womenfolk, after they've been together a while. Paper, cotton, leather, linen, automatic weapons.

Just kidding! That was a joke. It's just a handgun. The kind that fits in your purse. I have it in my purse right now.

> *(Point flashlight out into the audience at the purse in the playwright's lap. Give it a second.)*

Not really.

Inappropriate, I thought, even if this is a gun show.

> (Beat.)

What I'm saying is, this is a really big country. How often have YOU lived fifty miles away from law enforcement? Think about it. Have you ever?

Then what the fuck do you know about it, and why are you trying to take my fucking guns away?

"You can have my gun when you pry it out of my cold dead hands." John Milius. *Red Dawn*.

That's another good movie. Remember? Commies invade rural America.

A bunch of high school kids are forced to take up arms against them. Wolverines!! Patrick Swayze, C. Thomas Howell, Jennifer Grey, Charlie Sheen...

> (Beat.)

Can you believe Patrick Swayze is dead? God. Sometimes I feel old, just thinking of all the people who seemed like they could never die who are dead now. And if you're sitting there judging me because I put Patrick Swayze on that list, fuck you. He was fucking hot in *Dirty Dancing*.

Get back to the story, Ellen. Skip ahead.

> (Sound of a bell – the door at Jackson's Books closing.)

Not that far ahead.

> (Beat.)

Not that far ahead. We're not there yet. That's the third story.

> (Turn head away. Really long, awkward pause. Glance up.)

No, I didn't forget my next line.

> (Show script to an audience member and read from it.)

"Really long, awkward pause."

(Look over at the playwright in the audience.)

Who do you think you are, Pinter? Fucking playwrights.

(Beat; read from the script.)

There was something I was going to tell you, but I've... I've decided not to. Maybe I'll just...tell you four stories today.

(Beat; look at the playwright in the audience.)

If not now, when?

(Beat.)

Me learning to shoot, that's the second story.

I went shooting with Irwin out in the woods this one time. Back in Oregon. He wasn't my husband then. Not yet. But we'd been going out a while.

What? You didn't know I have a husband? I have a husband. His name is Irwin. Yes, really. He's a writer too, and he's part of this story.

(Take the picture of Irwin target shooting on the farm out of the box. Share it with the audience.)

It was this perfect Oregon day. You know? Like it was never going to rain again, it was that bright. But everything smelled green, and clean, because it had rained the night before. I was wearing a bikini top and short shorts and ear protection, and we had laid about twenty guns out on a blanket on the grass.

We were down by the lake, on Irwin's folks' place. An old gravel pit, really, but if you dig a hole in Oregon, it's going to fill up with water. Sun glimmered on the water. They'd built a little shooting range down there, years before, against the hillside. Bullet casings were scattered around. Old, ragged paper targets.

Sound of crickets.

We were the only two people in the universe.

Clean, heady smell of his sweat.

I'd never smelled that smell from that close up before.

Irwin was teaching me how to shoot, the real deal, never point your gun at something you don't want dead, telling me where the safety was. We were only drinking a little bit. Only beer.

He put his arms around me and showed me how to focus on the front sight, breathe out, and squeeze the trigger gently. Handguns. Rifles. His grandfather's gun. Guns he bought while he was in the Marines. Did I tell you he was a Marine? Oorah, baby. Semper Fi.

I remember that day so clearly. It was so goddamn fun.

He knew what he was doing, and what he was doing was strong and masculine and dangerous, and he was letting me in on it, he was giving that to me.

Focus on the front sight.

Breathe out.

Squeeze the trigger gently.

It was louder than anything I'd ever heard before. You nestle the butt of the rifle right up against your shoulder, right here, because it kicks when it fires.

We must have gone through two or three hundred rounds of ammunition that day, and a six-pack or two, in no particular hurry.

That day is bright and perfect in my memory.

Nobody ever made me feel safe like he made me feel safe.

That's the second story.

> *(Take the shirt out of the box – a man's shirt, soft and worn.)*

Raise your hand right now if you've ever held a gun in your hands. If you've ever gone shooting.

(Look around at the people who have raised their hands, and not raised their hands.)

If you haven't, you don't know how much fun it can be.

(Smell the shirt. Take a moment.)

Here's the third story. Move along, Ellen.

(Put the shirt back in the box.)

I was working at Jackson's Books. Small, independent bookstore in Salem, Oregon.

(Turn to the Jackson's Books story in the script. Remember.)

This is how it goes.

It's night.

It's quiet.

Me and Lauri look in cookbooks for good lasagne recipes.

Some lady calls up. This lady, she's in some contest. A treasure hunt. The question is, "Who wrote 'Pachelbel's Canon'?" So I say it's probably like, "Who's buried in Grant's tomb," but she's not easy about it. "Call me back," I say. "I'll look."

Lauri starts talking some blue-hair into Dostoevsky, I'm sitting on the floor in the music section, and this older guy comes in. And I say, "May I help you?"

He shakes his head and rubs his hands together.

Lauri wraps Fyodor up in blue paper behind the counter.

My guy looks a little lost over in Lit. Crit., so I say, "Is there anything I can help you find?"

"Is there anything you got in horr..." he says.

"Excuse me?" I say.

"Horrerrrr," he says a little louder. "Horror."

"Oh, sure," I say.

He's not telling any names, so I say, "How about Stephen King?" I hand him *Misery*, and *It*.

He thumbs through them kind of fast, like he's forgot his glasses. Blue-hair's gathering her stuff.

"You got...um...*Flowers in the Attic*, something like that?" he says.

"V.C. Andrews," I say. "Right down here."

The door clangs shut.

> *(That bell again – the sound of the door closing.)*

"I'll take them," he says, handing me all three of the paperbacks.

I go around the side of the counter. Lauri's still standing over at the other register. I scan each of the books, then look at the total. It says $14.97.

"Fourteen ninety-seven," I say, and look up.

And there is a really big black gun pointed at me.

Well, I really can't say how big it was. It looked like a bazillion caliber gun with its opening pointed right toward me. The cops told me later, laughing, any gun that's pointed at you looks big.

I just stood there. One hand poised over the register, the other hovering over the books on the counter.

Looking back now, my memory moves me in and out of my body – you know, like those dreams where you're watching somebody for a while, doing things, and then you *are* them. At this point, my memory slips me out from the body that sees that gun pointed at me to some place hovering up above and watching. And the expression that girl (who is me) has on her face is just like that big-eyed look that deers have when they're caught, for that one horrible moment, in your headlights.

"...Down on the floor," you hear him say. He's looking at Lauri.

"Down on the floor. Get down on the floor." By the third time he says this, he's shouting.

Lauri is just standing there, with those same deer eyes I have. Come to find out later, she couldn't even see the gun, with all the stuff on the counter. She did know though. She didn't understand what was going on, but she knew.

Lauri tells you later that you told her "It's okay" at this point, and that it was only when you said that to her that she crouched down behind the counter. She curled her arms around herself, like a kid under a desk when the bomb siren goes off.

"Get the money out of the register," he says to you. "Get The Money Out Of The Register! GET THE MONEY OUT OF THE REGISTER!!"

He pulls a crumpled brown paper bag out of his jacket and throws it on the counter. It slides across, and falls lightly to the floor.

"Get the bag – Get The Bag – GET THE BAG," he says, and his eyes are wide and fierce and the gun is pointed at you still.

You feel yourself moving, looking down at Lauri, picking up the bag.

The drawers at Jackson's won't come open again if you shut them, so they are always left ajar. We are woefully unprepared for this. You pull out the drawer in front of you.

Your fingernails slip on the bills in the cash register and you can't get hold of them.

"HurryupHurryUpHURRYUP!!" the man shouts.

You get your fingers around the corners of the bills, somehow, your fingernails making scraping sounds on the paper, and you think, "My God, I'm going to be killed because I didn't cut my fingernails."

You put the money in the bag and you put the bag on the counter and he shoves the bag back toward you.

"Gettheotherregister! GetTheOther..."

You step around Lauri, careful not to step on her hands, which she has set on the ground in front of her to keep her balance.

The man's hands are shaking, as he holds the gun, and as you empty the second register, you understand that if he doesn't shoot you on purpose, he may just shoot you accidentally. There is a tightness in your throat. Your own hands begin to shake, almost uncontrollably.

You push the bag of cash toward him, and he shoves it in his jacket.

He gestures at you with the gun.

You back away from the counter.

"Down on the floor. Down On The Floor. Get DOWN ON THE FLOOR!"

You get down on the floor, on your knees, on the dirty gray carpet.

The man's voice comes from the other side. "You count to a hundred," he says.

After a pause, you hear the door fall shut.

I still don't know who moved first, but then you and Lauri are grasping each other's hands, and I have never felt so close to anyone in my life as in that moment.

We don't count, but a little after the door sounds like it closes, we look at each other, then cautiously get up, peering over the counter. There is a man there, but it is just some guy with brown hair and loafers, paging through a book from the "New Non-Fiction" display by the door. I guess he doesn't notice the two of us, rising up from behind the counter like ghosts.

Things get kind of fuzzy, there for a while. I sit down on the stool behind the counter.

Lauri asks the man in the loafers if he saw the guy who just went out. The guy had no clue what had just happened. He was shocked. He'd passed right by the man, not even knowing it.

Lauri does all the right things. Locking the front door and calling the police. She had been a bank teller, and had the training.

I just sit there, kind of breathless.

The police come. Neither of the owners were home when Lauri called, but the manager and her husband come. Her husband is a retired English professor, and he keeps asking you questions like Columbo or Poirot, "Did he give off any peculiar smells? Did he have a tattoo?" even after the police stop.

The policeman is standing beside me, though, when I see my husband, framed in the glass doorway. He has a rose in rumpled green paper in one hand, and a box from the lingerie place in the other. Because it is my birthday. I am twenty-five.

There is a blank look in Irwin's eyes, as he pauses there in the doorway, waiting for Lauri to unlock it with her jingling ring of keys, knowing that something has gone wrong. I look over the shoulder of the policeman at him apologetically.

You finally get to sleep that night after the sun comes up. After getting drinks at Thompson's with Lauri, just till you quit shaking so bad. Irwin says it's the adrenaline – it's natural.

People say kind things and they say awful things. You remember the awful things best. Your boss, who has been taking judo with his sons at the same place you learned the little bit you know, asks you if you thought of using it, when "it happened." You want to bash his face in. It increases the guilt you feel that you could let this happen to you. One of the girls we work with tells Lauri, when Lauri says how afraid she is that the man is out there still, that "it's not like he raped you or anything." Lauri goes in the back, into the bathroom, and cries.

You go on, though. You keep working the evening shift, even though your mind goes back to that, now. The robbery. And it is harder to be friendly to strangers. You had sometimes been afraid, before, and now you are, sometimes, not afraid. You do go on, though.

But as you write this, putting words to paper, words run through your head.

I will never be the same.

I will never be the same.

I will never be the same.

That was the third story.

Note that no bookstore cashiers were actually hurt during this incident.

> *(Take the picture of young Ellen in her Jackson's Books days and share it.)*

Everybody was fine. I'm totally fine.

I'm totally fine. So what makes me feel like I need to stand up here and talk about this?

All you're seeing are the freaks. All anybody is seeing on the news are the freaks, people who really DO want to take all the guns away, or flag-draped yahoos like Alex Jones, when the reality is...much more complicated.

Somewhere between forty and forty-five percent of all households in America own guns, and they're not all nutcases who secretly want to gun us all down in a movie theater or an office building or a grade school. Somewhere between fifty-five and sixty percent of all households in America DON'T own guns, and they're not all pansy-ass granola-eating hippies who would rather stand and watch their family raped and killed than defend themselves.

There is a conversation to be had, here, that's not happening. It's been stolen from us sensible, relatively reasonable, regular sort of people in the middle, and the middle is bigger than the edges, we are way bigger than them, they just strut better, like fucking peacocks. But I aim to take this conversation BACK, because it belongs to us, all of us. And I refuse to cede this ground to the nutjobs who don't want to let us talk to each other, because we're the kind of people who might admit that this issue has just a little bit of fucking complexity to it. And that we have more in common with each other than we have that separates us.

We are human. We breathe air. We live in the world. We eat, we drink, we require shelter. We crave companionship. We build families.

We want to be SAFE.

I've been thinking about this gun thing a lot, circling around it.

And what I think it comes down to, this gun thing, is safety. That's what we have in common. We want to be *safe*.

(Pause.)

Fourth story.

(Take out the New York City subway map.)

So I've just moved to New Jersey from Los Angeles, where there is no public transportation – well, no public transportation that makes a dent in the vast distances you're always having to go. It's fifty-five miles across, the city of Los Angeles, did you know that? Manhattan is two point three miles across.

I've moved to New Jersey, but today I've taken the train into New York City, which feels much more like a city than Los Angeles ever will, and I've spent the day there, getting lost no fewer than three times, and looking at my little map like the newbie I am.

It's dark and rainy and cold out, and I'm exhausted, and it's late, and I'm in Pennsylvania Station, which smells like urine and is constantly, constantly under construction. I'm looking for New Jersey Transit, because I know that's what I need to get home.

There are these two cops standing there in the station, and so I go over and ask them which way to the New Jersey Transit trains. And the big, broad-shouldered, white cop, whose hand rests firmly and comfortably on his sidearm, says, "I'm gonna pistol-whip the next asshole from New Jersey who fuckin' asks me that, read the fuckin' signs." And the big, broad-shouldered, younger Latino cop standing beside him doesn't say anything.

The cop's hand doesn't move from his sidearm. His hand doesn't move. But I am suddenly aware of his hand, resting firmly and comfortably on the butt of his gun, the silver snap on the black leather holster that can be flicked open with his thumb as he draws the gun out of the holster, and he doesn't do that, he doesn't, but I'm very aware of his large, calloused hand.

    (Beat.)

He never would have said that to me if I was…if I was with Irwin.

    (Beat.)

Funny thing, how if you have a gun, your tendency is to use it.

    (Beat; tilt head. No, that's not right.)

He didn't use it. He didn't draw. He didn't fire. He just…

They always say that thing, though. And I think there's something to it. If you ask a pharmacist what to do, they'll prescribe a pill. If you ask a surgeon, the only thing to do is cut it out. If you have a gun…

> (Beat.)

It wasn't really even a threat. Not really. He didn't move when he said it. But I guess it's another one of my gun stories.

I found New Jersey on my own.

I like cops. My uncle is a cop. Cops make me feel...

> (Pause.)

One more story.

> (Beat.)

Do I tell it?

> (Beat.)

Do I tell it?

> *(Glance over at the playwright in the audience.)*

Maybe every storyteller has one story they hold on to. The story they don't let go, or the story that doesn't let go of them. But I think maybe it's time to shake this one loose.

Something happened *[number of years since April 27, 2003]* years ago. April 27, 2003.

This is the first story, this is the last story, this is the only story.

> *(Take Ellen and Irwin's wedding picture out of the box and look at it. Smile. Remember. Let this story be happy until it isn't, okay?)*

Irwin and I were the only married couple in our grad school writing program. You remember Irwin from the Learning to Shoot story, right? Met him when I was nineteen and he was twenty-nine, and everything was shining ahead of us. Met him and married him back in Oregon, then went off to grad school together to be Writers, capital W. And everybody in our program would come over to our place, and I'd cook, and we'd drink, and we'd share our writing and talk long into the night, like grad school is supposed to go. Then grad school was done with, and we went out into the real world. And he got a crazy job in the internet boom just in time to ride it all the way up...then all the way back down to the internet bust. And I found a job just as we were getting to absolute zero, but he didn't. And he didn't. And he didn't. And he kind of stopped looking after a while, and he got kind of anxious and depressed.

(Beat.)

Irwin's the toughest guy I ever met, Marine Corps, oorah, put himself through college working as a correctional officer, ran a marathon, tough, and he's always the funniest guy in any room he's in. He's the fucking sun, and most of the time I was happy to be a planet, because of the brightness and the warmth. He's the toughest guy I ever met. So it took about two years of shrinks and pills and VA counselors and sometimes walking all night together through the Los Angeles dark, where there are no stars, only airplanes, because he was feeling nervous, all of which we didn't really tell anybody about, because he didn't want anybody to know –

– Shh! Don't tell anybody, don't tell anybody, don't tell anybody, don't leave me, don't let them take me away some place, don't you fucking tell anybody, please don't leave, baby, shh!

– Before he took a beautiful shiny black Glock and put it in his mouth and pulled the trigger. And when I found him, he was...

And when I found him, he was...

There's not really any doubt when someone uses a gun. Because you can see that he's... Blood on the...concrete floor of the...not-blood on the... Red and gray. Red and gray. Red and gray. I put my hand on his chest. I put my ear to his chest, too...because...I, uh...couldn't... I still can't, really...believe that...

(Pause.)

He was really funny. You would have liked him.

>*(Pause; put hands on table.)*

So that's it. There's my five stories. There's my gun show.

>*(Turn the page – but instead of it saying "end of play," there is more text there.)*

No.

> *(Show audience page that says "no" in big letters.)*

That's not it. That's not the whole story.

I'm...stuck. I'm stuck.

> *(Beat.)*

I'm the kind of widow you don't talk about, because there's a shame in suicide. There's a god-awful guilt, because if you love someone, you're not supposed to let him down, and if he's dead...

You failed.

But if we don't talk about this, if we don't talk about suicide, we're skipping a huge part of the story. The guns-make-you-safe story.

> *(Beat.)*

Thirty thousand, one hundred and thirty-five people were killed with firearms in 2003. Plus one. Thirty thousand, one hundred and thirty-six.

> *(Touch picture of Ellen and Irwin.)*

I don't want to take everybody's guns away. But I sure wish I'd manned up and taken his guns away.

> *(Beat.)*

We have met the enemy, and he is us.

> *(Beat.)*

All the people I know who have died from guns killed themselves.

- Mr. Stone, my high school biology teacher.
- Kid I went to catechism classes with, who also happened to be my seventh-grade teacher's son.
- Ron, a friend of my aunt and uncle.
- Richard's dad.
- Irwin.
- Hunter S. Thompson.

- Ernest Hemingway.

And don't you try to tell me I can't have those last couple guys because I didn't know them, I fucking love those guys.

Is my list shorter or longer than yours?

I don't know anybody who has ever drawn a gun to protect themselves. Maybe my father-in-law did, in Korea. I don't know. He doesn't talk about it.

If help is an hour away and you don't have a gun to protect yourself against someone who does, you're fucked. But if there's a gun in your house, you're more likely to shoot yourself with it than protect yourself with it. Complicated.

Guns don't equal safety.

"No guns" doesn't equal safety.

There is no fucking safety.

> (Beat.)

I never tell this story. It's an ugly story. Complicated. Messy. Violent. *[Number of years since April 27, 2003]* years, I've clutched it tight. Held it inside me.

I shoved both of us in a box and put us away. And now it's *[number of years since April 27, 2003]* years later, and here we are. Still in the same box I put us in. I can put us back in. I can do it. I'm good at this. But that doesn't get us anywhere, does it?

> (A moment.)

Irwin and I are locked together forever. Death didn't part us. For *[number of years since April 27, 2003]* years, I've held him tight and close, right here.

> (Clench fist and press it against side, against the lowest and most vulnerable ribs.)

The tighter my hold, the more caught I am.

It's like how you catch a monkey. I read about this somewhere. It's easy. Apparently. I've never been to any place with wild monkeys to try it out. But they say that all you have to do is drill a small hole in a gourd and tie it to a tree. Put a piece of fruit inside. Then come back later to see if you've caught one. What happens is they smell the sweet fruit and stick their hand through the hole and grab it. Their little fists won't fit back through the hole, but they won't let go. You can go back any time you want. They'll still be there, clutching tight. You can just scoop them up in a bag, and there you go.

We have guns, and the guns have us, here in America. We're scooping ourselves up in shiny black body bags.

I don't want to be locked together anymore.

I kept the gun Irwin gave me. But I DON'T WANT THIS FUCKING GIFT. Carrying it all this time, carrying. I kept his name. I kept his things, safely packed up in boxes, his things and my things and our things. I kept his note. "Love you always." I kept his gun. It isn't in this box.

DUMP BOX OUT ON FLOOR.

>   *(Shake head "no" at this.)*

No.

It isn't in this box. I've carried it much closer all this time. I carried it here, right here – BUT I DON'T WANT THIS GIFT.

>   *(Quick shift; look out at the playwright in the audience.)*

This feels incredibly disloyal, this...

>   *(Make ripping gesture.)*

Stuck in the middle with you.

>   *(Turn the page of the script, read stage direction.)*

No, really. Dump out the box.

(Show stage direction to audience, then violently dump box out on floor.)

This is a show about guns.

I may have gotten distracted, but I didn't forget.

You're just as stuck as I am, America. You, America. Us, America. In love with something that's hurting us and not sure how to separate it from our identity. America means freedom and liberty and self-determination and independence, and guns were a tool we used to get those things, one of the tools, they were, but they weren't the point. The *freedom* was the point. And I don't think we're very free right now.

We're afraid. All of us. And we aren't talking to each other.

If you're on the right, do you feel like you can talk about a few simple, practical things we might want to do to keep guns out of the hands of people who shouldn't have them – like three-year-olds and convicted felons and maybe the mentally ill? Or is that unacceptable? Who says?

If you're on the left, do you feel like you can talk about the times and places where guns might be a practical tool for hunting or self-defense? Or even just fun, like some of the other dangerous things we love sometimes? Or is that unacceptable? Who says?

Can we have this conversation? If not, why not? What's stopping us from figuring this out? I know it's complicated. But we are in this together. This country. This society. This community.

Me and Irwin's story is just one story, one gun story in a country full of gun stories and a lot of them are a lot more…but this one is mine. And I don't want to be silent about it anymore. I failed before. I don't want to fail again. So I'm not going to put us back in the box.

(Kick the box. A moment.)

I haven't given you a plan, here tonight. I haven't given you a set of actions to be taken or congressmen to be called or protests to carry signs at.

All I have to give you is the story I never tell.

> *(Pick up script and hand several pages out to random audience members.)*

Here.

Here.

If I give our story out to enough people, maybe I'll never be able to put us back in.

Take this.

Take it, goddamn it.

> *(Throw the rest of the pages of the script up into the air so they flutter down slowly across the stage.)*
>
> *(Exit.)*
>
> *(There is a long moment of empty, lit stage. Then the lights go out.)*

End of Play

PROPS

Duo Version
- A copy of the script.
- A really strong flashlight, like a cop carries.
- A box of photos and other remembrances, closed up with tape. There should be a variety of items in the box – eclectic personal items that a man might keep on his desk or on his dresser, including a man's shirt.

Several photos will be taken out of the box and shared during the course of the play:

- A photo of Ellen's childhood home on the farm for the Growing Up with Guns in Oregon story.
- A photo of Irwin on the farm for the Learning to Shoot story.
- A photo of young Ellen, alive and well, for the Jackson's Books story.
- A New York City subway map for the Penn Station story.
- A framed photograph of the playwright and her husband at their wedding for the Last story.

Solo Version
- A copy of the script.
- A box of photos and other remembrances, closed up with tape. There should be a variety of items in the box – eclectic personal items that a man might keep on his desk or on his dresser, including a man's shirt.

Several photos will be taken out of the box and shared during the course of the play:

- A picture of the playwright (E. M. Lewis).
- A photo of Ellen's childhood home on the farm for the Growing Up with Guns in Oregon story.
- A photo of Irwin on the farm for the Learning to Shoot story.
- A photo of young Ellen, alive and well, for the Jackson's Books story.
- A New York City subway map for the Penn Station story.
- A framed photograph of the playwright and her husband at their wedding for the Last story.

www.ingramcontent.com/pod-product-compliance
Lightning Source LLC
Chambersburg PA
CBHW050303010526
44108CB00040B/2243